Cats and Dogs

Illustrated by
Robin Lee Makowski

cover photo © Image Source Limited

Visit us at www.kidsbooks.com

INTRODUCTION

This book will teach you how to draw many different types of cats and dogs. Some are more difficult to draw than others, but if you follow along, step by step, then (most important!) practice on your own, you soon will be able to draw these adorable animals. You also will learn methods for drawing anything that you want by breaking it down into basic shapes.

The most basic and commonly used shape is the oval. There are many variations of ovals: some are small and almost round, others are long and narrow, many are in between.

Most of the figures in this book begin with some kind of oval. Then other shapes and lines are added to it to form the basic animal outline. Most times, a free-form oval is used, like the ones pictured below.

In addition to ovals, variations of other basic shapes—such as circles, squares, rectangles, and triangles—plus simple lines, are used to connect the shapes. You will use these basic shapes to start your drawing.

Some basic oval and free-form shapes:

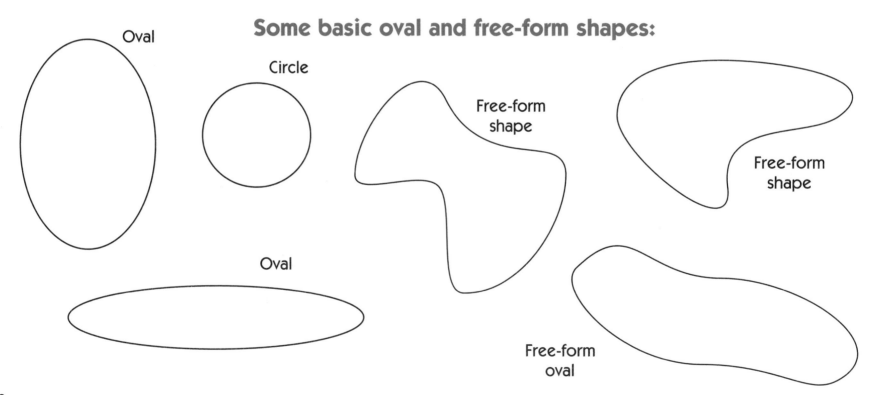

Oval

Circle

Free-form shape

Free-form shape

Oval

Free-form oval

SUPPLIES

NUMBER-2 PENCILS   FELT-TIP PEN
SOFT ERASER   COLORED PENCILS
DRAWING PAD   MARKERS OR CRAYONS

HELPFUL HINTS

1. Take your time with steps 1 and 2. Following the first steps carefully will make the final steps easier. The first two steps create a solid foundation of the figure, much like a builder who must construct a foundation before constructing the rest of the house. Next comes the fun part—creating a smooth, clean outline drawing of the animal, then adding all the finishing touches, such as details, shading, and color.

2. Always keep your pencil lines light and soft. This will make the guidelines easier to erase when you no longer need them.

3. Don't be afraid to erase. It usually takes a lot of sketching and erasing before you will be satisfied with the way your drawing looks.

4. Add details, shading, and all the finishing touches only *after* you have blended and refined all the shapes and your figure is complete.

5. Remember: Practice makes perfect. Don't be discouraged if you don't get the hang of it right away. Just keep drawing, erasing, and redrawing until you do.

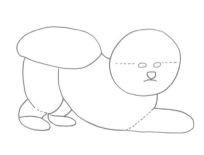

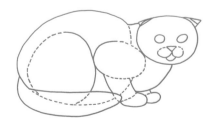

HOW TO START

First, study the finished drawing, number 4, below. Then study the steps that were taken to get to that final drawing. Notice where the shapes overlap and where they align. Is the eye over the corner of the mouth or behind it? Look for relationships among the shapes.

Sometimes, it is helpful to start by tracing the final drawing. This will give you a sense of the overall body shape, as well as which basic shapes are where. This will make it easier for you to draw the animal from scratch.

Step 1. Draw the main shape first—usually, it is the largest. In this case, it is a large oval for the body. Then, for this cat, add smaller basic shapes: ovals for the chest, head, eyes, and feet; triangles for the ears; and curving lines for legs and tail.

Step 2. Sketch and erase to reshape the head and body. As you work, erase guidelines that you no longer need. Blend and refine the shapes to create a smooth outline of the body.

Note: Dotted lines show guidelines that you will erase when you no longer need them (in this case, in step 2).

Step 3. Start adding details—to the face, ears, and body, for example. Again, use simple lines and shapes—for the pupils of this cat's eyes, for instance. Keep sketching and erasing until you are satisfied.

Step 4. Now add the final details, such as shading. Note how lots of short, choppy lines give a sense of fur texture. If you wish, add color using colored pencils, markers, or crayons.

Remember: It is not important to get it perfect. It *is* important for you to be happy with your work!

Erasing Tips
- Once you have completed the line drawing (usually after step 2), erase unneeded guidelines. Then add details, shading, and/or coloring to your drawing.
- In the final stages, you may use a felt-tip marker over pencil lines that you want to keep. This will make it easier to erase unneeded pencil lines.
- A very soft or kneaded eraser will erase the pencil lines without smudging the drawing or ripping the paper.

1.
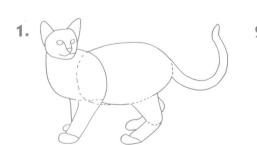

2.
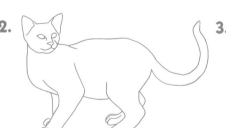

3.
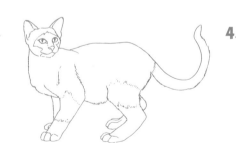

4.

FUR REAL!

How to Draw Cats and Dogs would not be complete without a lesson on how to draw fur. It is not that hard to do if you follow these instructions and use the tips and tricks. It does take a little time to make a drawing look good, however, so be patient and practice, practice, practice!

Tip #1: Draw fur in the direction in which it grows. This will add volume and dimension to your drawing.

Wrong: Straight, single-direction lines make the shape look flat.

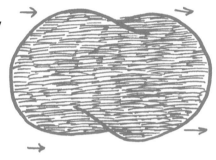

Right: This is the same shape, but the fur lines are drawn along the contour of the shape, to flow in the same direction.

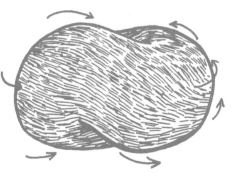

Tip #2: Practice drawing "hair balls"—try sketching both long hair and short hair on flat circles, to learn how to turn them into fuzzy, 3-D balls.

Tip #3: If you have a pet cat or dog, study it carefully. Notice how the fur grows, where it turns, and where it gets longer or shorter.

PARTS OF A DOG OR CAT

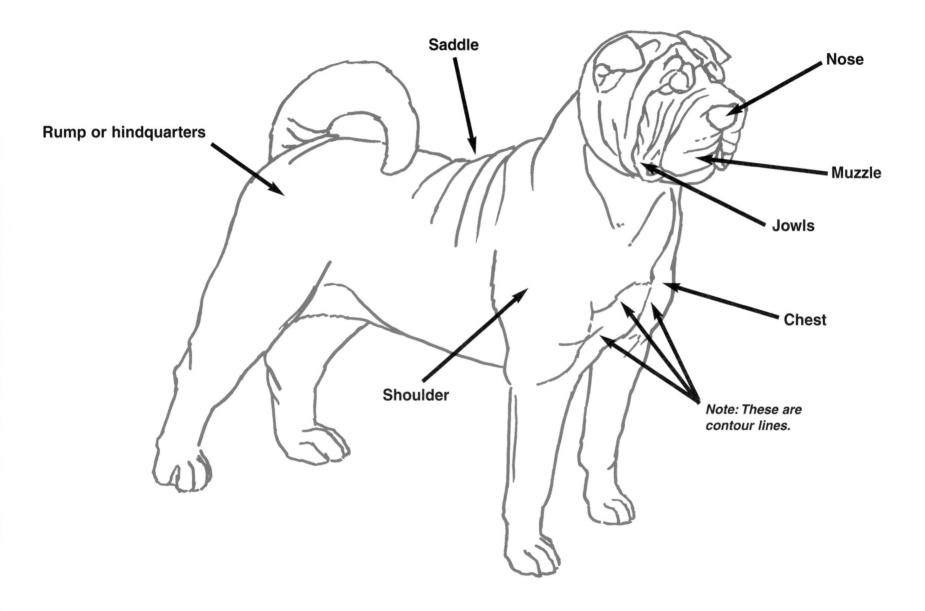

Saddle

Nose

Rump or hindquarters

Muzzle

Jowls

Chest

Shoulder

Note: These are contour lines.

Sphynx

Sphynx cats have such short hair that they look hairless! They are affectionate and get along well with other pets.

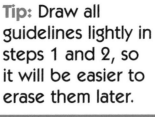

Tip: Draw all guidelines lightly in steps 1 and 2, so it will be easier to erase them later.

1. Begin by sketching a large, blocklike shape for the chest. Add an oval for the head, then add the ears, eyes, and muzzle. Sketch the free-form shapes for the body and hindquarters. Then add the legs, paws, and tail.

2. Sketch and erase to blend the shapes into a smooth outline, erasing lines you no longer need. Refine the facial features and add toes.

3. Draw the head, neck, and leg wrinkles. Darken the nose and lightly shade in the ears and lower body.

Coloring: The sphynx cat is white, black, tan, or gray.

Angora

This breed of cat originated in Turkey. Angoras are intelligent and make loving and devoted pets.

1. Start with large free-form shapes for the body and chest. Add ovals for the head, snout, and eyes, and triangles for the ears. Then sketch in simple guideline shapes for the legs, feet, and bushy tail.

2. Sketching and erasing, blend the shapes into a smooth body shape. Add jagged lines to create fur at the large neck ruff. Then refine the facial features and the paws.

Tip: It will be easier to draw almost anything if you first break it down into simple shapes.

3. Use short, choppy strokes to make the edges of the fur look fuzzy. Further define the facial features. Do not go on to the last step until you are happy with your drawing at this stage.

4. Use long strokes to add fur all over the head and body. Keep the patches on the head, chest, and legs white. Don't forget to add the whiskers! Complete your drawing by adding the finishing touches.

Coloring: Classic Angora cats are white, but this breed can be any color.

Tortoiseshell

The word *tortoiseshell* is used to describe cats that have fur with random patches of orange, black, and cream.

1. Sketch large free-form shapes for the chest and body. Add an oval for the head, then add simple shapes for the muzzle, eyes, and ears. Then sketch in the tail and paws.

2. Blend the shapes into a clean outline of this cat's body, erasing lines you no longer need. Shape the muzzle, eyes, and ears.

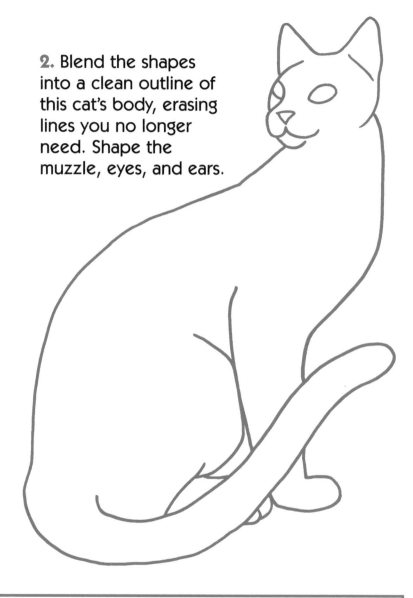

Tip: No one gets it right the first time. Erasing and redrawing are important parts of the process.

3. Sketch the patches on the face and body, as shown. Darken the eyes and add the toes.

4. With a marker, use short strokes to add the fur pattern to the patches. When you have one layer stroked in, go back and add a few darker lines throughout the patches to complete the pattern. Leave the rest of the cat white.

Coloring: The tortoiseshell pattern can be shades of black, tan, rust, and brown. In a number of breeds, the pattern covers the whole cat.

Turkish Van

This breed originated in Turkey. Turkish Vans are affectionate and love to play. They also like to swim!

1. Start with a large free-form shape for the hindquarters. Draw an oval for the upper body, then a diamond-shaped head. Add the eyes, nose, and pointy ears, then the legs and the large, bushy tail.

2. Sketch and erase to blend the shapes and define the face. Add the mouth. This breed is very fluffy, so use squiggly lines to make the edges of the fur look fuzzy.

Note: If something seems complex, focus on one part at a time. Look for simple lines and shapes that will be easier to draw.

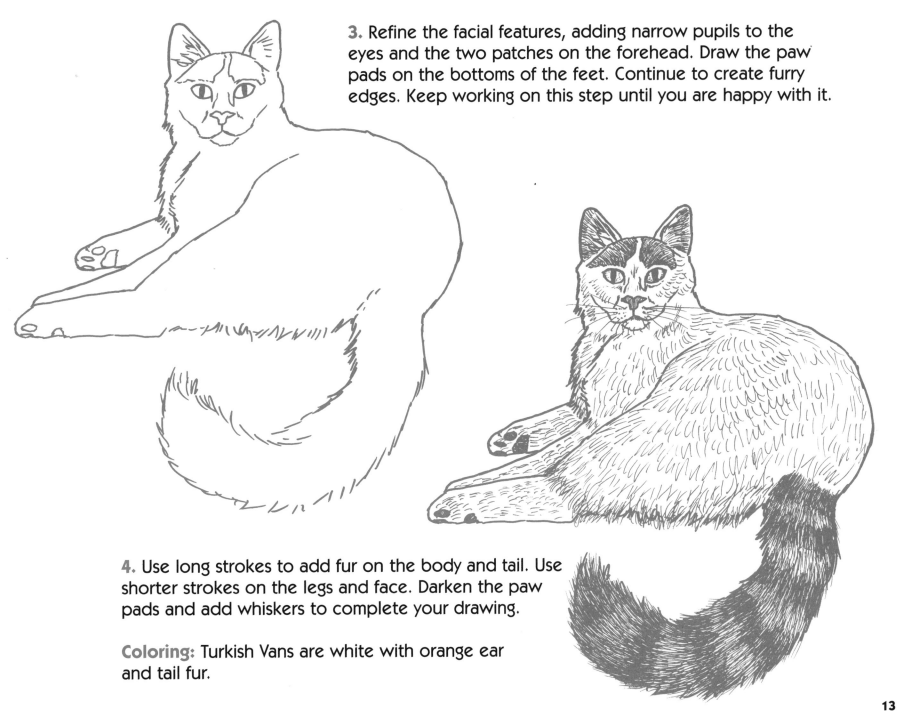

3. Refine the facial features, adding narrow pupils to the eyes and the two patches on the forehead. Draw the paw pads on the bottoms of the feet. Continue to create furry edges. Keep working on this step until you are happy with it.

4. Use long strokes to add fur on the body and tail. Use shorter strokes on the legs and face. Darken the paw pads and add whiskers to complete your drawing.

Coloring: Turkish Vans are white with orange ear and tail fur.

Devon Rex

This rare and unusual cat comes from England and has curly fur.

1. Sketch a large, free-form shape for the body, then an oval for the head. Add the eyes, muzzle, and the triangular ears. Add the legs and the tail.

2. Blend the shapes, erasing any lines you no longer need. Define the facial features. Don't go on to step 3 until you are satisfied with your step 2 drawing.

Tip: Usually, starting a drawing is easier if you sketch the largest shape first.

3. Continue to refine the ears and facial features. The Devon rex has a thick, soft, curly coat that waves in layers. Create the fur using short strokes on the face and body as shown. Don't forget to add the toes.

4. Continue to add fur details using short, tight strokes. Darken the nose and ears and add the finishing details.

Coloring: The Devon rex can be almost any color or pattern.

Longhaired Silver Tabby

This spectacular-looking cat has a silvery undercoat with black tabby stripes on top. The stripes are slightly blurred, due to the extra-long fur.

2. Use short strokes to create fur for this tabby. Add the pupils and darken the outline of the eyes. Sketch and erase to refine the shape of the muzzle and nose.

1. Begin with a rectangular head. Draw shapes for the slanted eyes, the nose, and the muzzle. Add small triangular ears. Then sketch in the neck ruff.

Tip: Keep all your lines and shapes lightly drawn until the final step.

3. Use long, loose strokes to detail the fur. Darken the nose and add the whiskers. With a few finishing touches, your portrait is complete.

Coloring: The silver tabby is silvery gray. You can use light blue and lavender for highlights and shading.

Abyssinian

Each hair of an Abyssinian's fur is several different colors. It starts silvery, then gradually changes from brown to black.

1. Sketch a large free-form shape for this breed's slender body. Next, draw an oval for the head. Add eyes, ears, and muzzle. Then sketch the legs, paws, and long tail.

2. Blend the shapes into a smooth body outline, erasing guidelines that you no longer need. Define the facial features and draw the pupils. Add the toes.

Tip: Add details and finishing touches *after* your figure is complete.

3. Use light, short strokes to fill in the fur details. Use a heavier stroke on the neck and tail patterns. Then add the whiskers and other final touches.

Coloring: Abyssinians can be any color, but the markings are consistent in all members of the breed.

Manx

Manx cats have short, stubby tails. Although their fur is short, it is thicker than that of other shorthaired cats. The breed probably originated on the Isle of Man, a small island in the Irish Sea.

1. Start with a large, blocky body shape. Draw an overlapping oval for the head. Then add the eyes, nose, mouth, ears, legs, and stubby tail.

2. Blend and refine all the shapes into a smooth outline of the Manx. Erase guide-lines you no longer need.

Tip: If at this point you are not satisfied with any part of your drawing, erase it and start over.

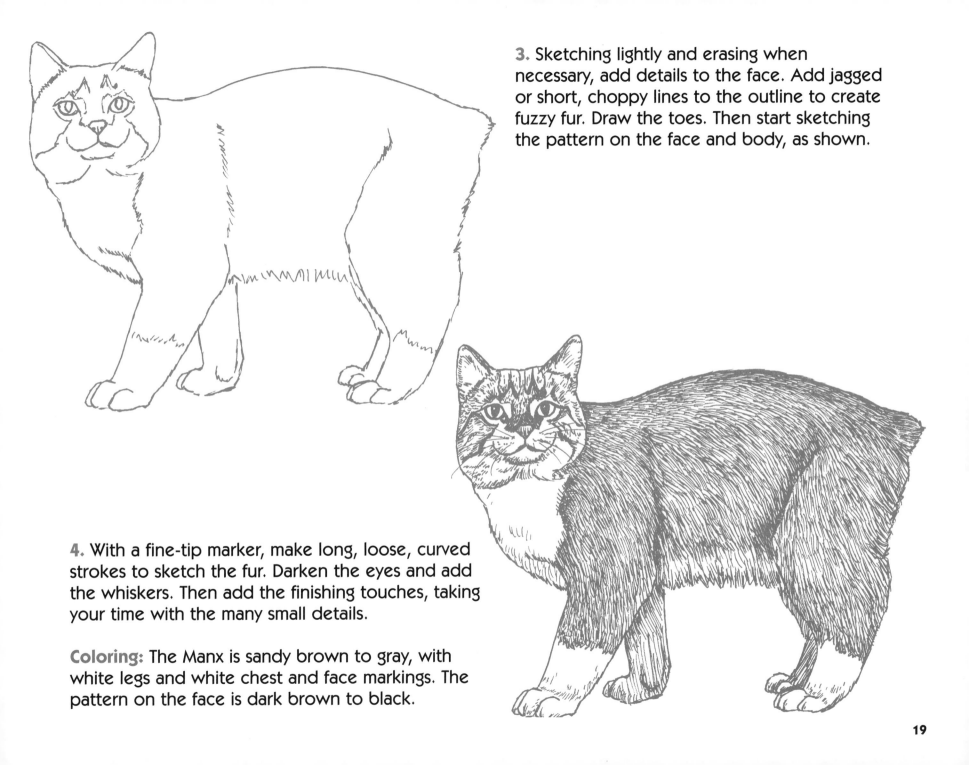

3. Sketching lightly and erasing when necessary, add details to the face. Add jagged or short, choppy lines to the outline to create fuzzy fur. Draw the toes. Then start sketching the pattern on the face and body, as shown.

4. With a fine-tip marker, make long, loose, curved strokes to sketch the fur. Darken the eyes and add the whiskers. Then add the finishing touches, taking your time with the many small details.

Coloring: The Manx is sandy brown to gray, with white legs and white chest and face markings. The pattern on the face is dark brown to black.

Korat

This breed of cat has been around since the 1800s. Korats are playful, intelligent, and very curious cats.

1. Start by drawing a large, free-form shape for the upper body, as shown. Add overlapping shapes for the head and hindquarters. Then sketch in guideline shapes for the eyes, muzzle, and ears. Add the legs, paws, and long tail.

2. Erasing unneeded lines and sketching new ones, blend the shapes and extend the front legs upward, as shown. Refine the facial features, then the ears and tail. Take your time with this step, working on one area at a time until you are satisfied with it.

Remember: Guidelines should always be drawn lightly. If you don't like the way something looks, erase it and try it again.

3. Using soft, light strokes, sketch the pattern around the eyes. Do the same—with the help of your eraser, too—to give the chest, legs, and tail a furry look.

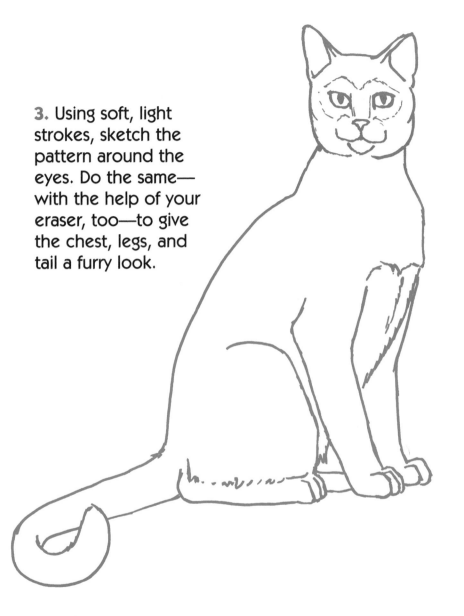

4. Use a lot of short strokes to add dark fur to the face and body. Use lighter, farther-apart strokes on the face, because this area is lighter. Don't forget the whiskers!

Coloring: Korats are a beautiful blue-gray color. If you are using crayons, use a light, medium-blue layer over the whole cat, then add a gray layer over it. Color the eyes green.

American Shorthair

American shorthairs are large, usually friendly, and gentle cats. Their good nature makes them popular as pets. Their fur can be any color or pattern.

1. Sketch a guideline shape for the head—narrow at the bottom, wide at the top. Add ears. Sketch shapes for the chest and hindquarters, then connect them. Next, add legs and tail, then sketch in guideline shapes for the eyes and muzzle.

2. Refine the eyes and muzzle, as shown. Sketch new lines and erase unneeded ones to combine all the shapes into a smooth outline. Add toes and paw pads on the two hind paws, and toes on the front paws.

Remember: Take your time with steps 1 and 2. If you get the foundation right, the rest of your drawing will be easier to do.

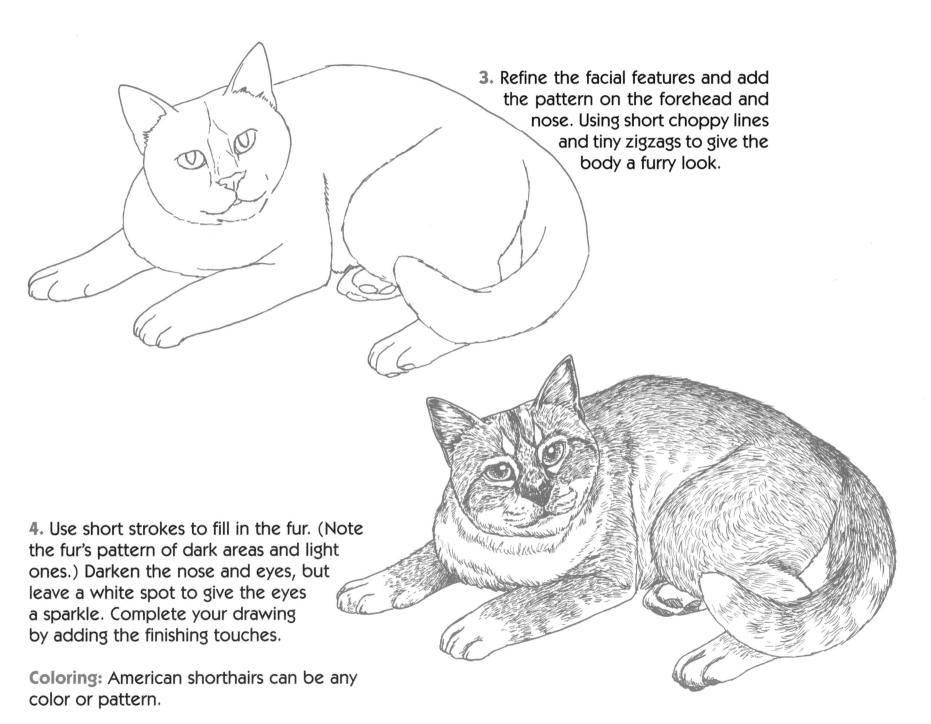

3. Refine the facial features and add the pattern on the forehead and nose. Using short choppy lines and tiny zigzags to give the body a furry look.

4. Use short strokes to fill in the fur. (Note the fur's pattern of dark areas and light ones.) Darken the nose and eyes, but leave a white spot to give the eyes a sparkle. Complete your drawing by adding the finishing touches.

Coloring: American shorthairs can be any color or pattern.

Siamese

Siamese cats have blue eyes and tan or cream-colored fur with a darker color on the face, ears, tail, and legs. These dark areas are called *points*. There are five types of points: blue, chocolate, seal (dark brown), lilac, and red (reddish orange). This popular breed originated in Thailand, once known as Siam.

1. Lightly sketch a large oval for the body. Draw smaller, overlapping shapes for the chest and head. Add eyes, nose, and mouth, then large pointy ears. Add the legs and the long, slender tail.

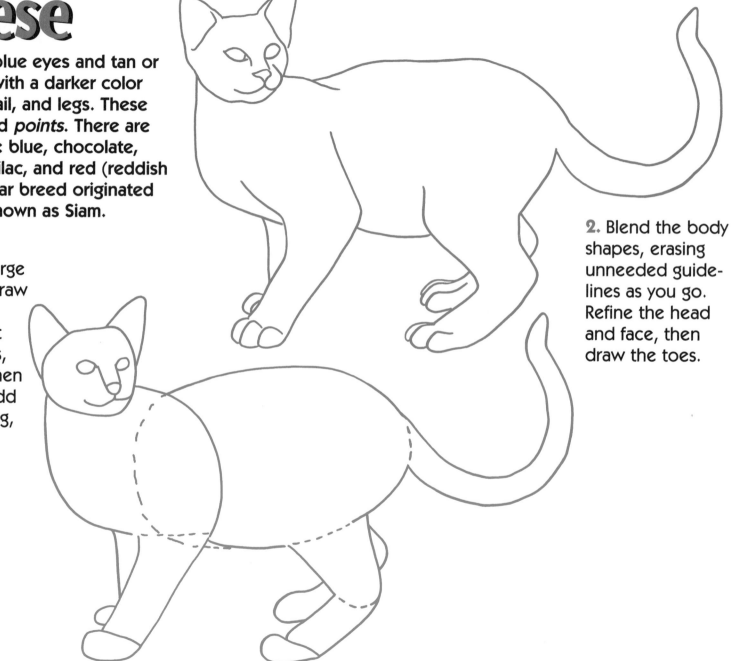

2. Blend the body shapes, erasing unneeded guidelines as you go. Refine the head and face, then draw the toes.

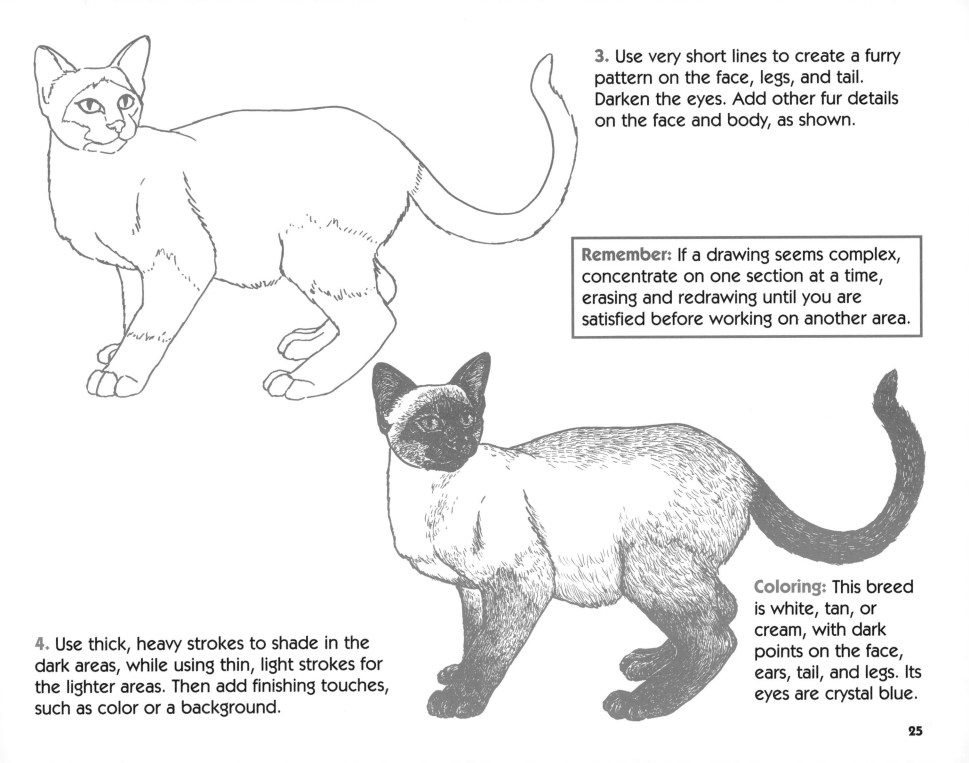

3. Use very short lines to create a furry pattern on the face, legs, and tail. Darken the eyes. Add other fur details on the face and body, as shown.

Remember: If a drawing seems complex, concentrate on one section at a time, erasing and redrawing until you are satisfied before working on another area.

4. Use thick, heavy strokes to shade in the dark areas, while using thin, light strokes for the lighter areas. Then add finishing touches, such as color or a background.

Coloring: This breed is white, tan, or cream, with dark points on the face, ears, tail, and legs. Its eyes are crystal blue.

25

Tabby Cat

The word *tabby* refers to the markings on the cat, not the purity of the breed, as commonly believed. Stripes are the main coat pattern among these cats, which can be of any breed.

2. Add pupils to the eyes. Sketch and erase to reshape and refine the other facial features, as shown. Create furry edges along the outline of the head.

1. Begin with a large oval for this tabby's face. Add guideline shapes for the eyes, nose, and mouth. Sketch in the large ears, then add lines for the neck.

3. Darken the outline of the eyes and pupils. Then draw in a pattern of stripes on the face and neck. Take your time, and don't be afraid to erase and try again.

4. Use short, heavy strokes to fill in the dark stripes, and use lighter, thinner strokes for the others. Add the whiskers and other finishing touches to complete your drawing.

Coloring: Tabbies can be many colors. The characteristic that makes a cat a tabby is the shape and pattern of the stripes.

Remember: Do not add final details or finishing touches until your main figure is complete and you are satisfied with it.

Kittens Playing

Kittens are very playful. They love to play with their owners, other kittens, and small, mobile objects. Playing helps kittens learn coordination and agility.

1. Draw one kitten at a time, starting each with the largest shape— the one for the body. Then add over- lapping guideline shapes for each kitten's head, ears, legs, and tail.

2. Take your time, lightly sketching and erasing to start refining the shape of each kitten's body, head, and tail. Add guideline shapes for the eyes and paws.

3. Blend each kitten's guideline shapes into a clean outline, erasing any lines you no longer need. Make sure that you are satisfied with your drawing of both kittens before going on to the final steps.

Remember: No one gets it right the first time! Practice makes perfect—so does erasing and trying again, when necessary.

Turn the page for the final steps for this drawing.

"Kittens Playing,"
continued from
pages 28-29

4. Use jagged or very short, choppy lines to give each kitten's outline a furry look, especially on the tails, as shown. Then start adding other details.

5. Sketch and erase to define and add details to each kitten's eye, ears, nose, and mouth. Create toes for each paw, adding claws or paw pads, where shown.

6. Use short strokes to draw fur all over these kittens' bodies. Then add the final details, paying special attention to the heads, faces, and paws. To complete your drawing, choose fur patterns or colorings from the breeds shown elsewhere in this book, or feel free to use your imagination.

Persian

This longhaired cat is known for its long, fluffy fur. It has a round face, round eyes, a snub nose, and small ears. The breed probably originated in Iran, a country once called Persia.

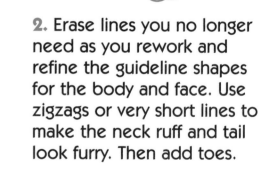

1. Start with a large oval for this cat's head and chest. Sketch guideline shapes for the facial features and ears. Draw the football-shaped body, then add the legs and the large, bushy tail.

2. Erase lines you no longer need as you rework and refine the guideline shapes for the body and face. Use zigzags or very short lines to make the neck ruff and tail look furry. Then add toes.

Tip: This cat may appear difficult to draw, but if you follow along carefully, step by step, you will be able to draw it. It takes patience, practice, and lots of erasing to get a drawing right.

3. Complete the facial features and add pupils to the eyes. Keep erasing and redrawing along all body and tail lines to refine this longhaired cat's furry outline

4. Use longer, looser strokes to fill in the fur on the body. (See page 5 for tips on giving the fur a realistic look.) Note that even the feet are furry on this cat! Don't forget the whiskers.

Coloring: Persian cats have fur of many different colors and patterns. Feel free to use your imagination for the final details.

Burmese

Burmese cats have a sweet nature and enjoy the company of humans. According to legend, they were used to guard religious temples in southeast Asia.

2. Sketch and erase to combine all the guideline shapes into a smooth outline. Define the ears and face. Draw the folds in this cat's skin. Don't forget to add the toes.

1. Begin with a large oval for the chest. Draw an overlapping oval for the head. Erase the first oval's guideline within the head shape, then sketch shapes for the eyes, muzzle, and triangular nose. Add the ears, legs, hindquarters, and tail.

Remember: Dotted lines represent guidelines that you will erase when you no longer need them.

3. Sketching lightly, create a furry look as you refine the overall outline of the cat. Add a fur pattern on the face, as shown. Then sketch in the claws.

4. Using a sharp pencil or fine-tip marker, make lots of short strokes to fill in this cat's short, smooth fur. Don't forget to add the long hairs sticking out of the ears. Darken the eyes and nose and, if you wish, color the body with a crayon or colored marker.

Coloring: A Burmese cat's fur is usually a rich shade of dark brown, and its eyes are yellow or golden orange.

Calico

A calico is defined by the color pattern of its fur: areas of orange, black, and cream (tortoiseshell) with large white patches. This cat, which can be short-haired or longhaired, is nearly always female.

1. Lightly draw ovals for the hindquarters, chest, and head. Add guideline shapes for the ears and facial features. Add the leg and tail.

2. Blend the shapes into a clean, smooth outline, erasing lines you no longer need. Refine the facial features and add the toes.

Remember: Take your time with steps 1 and 2. Getting the foundation right will make the picture easier to draw.

3. Complete the face, then start adding the distinct calico pattern on the saddle, tail, and face.

4. Use heavy strokes to fill in the dark patches of fur, and light strokes for the other areas. Leave the neck ruff, chest, and paws white. Darken the eyes and add the whiskers, and you're done!

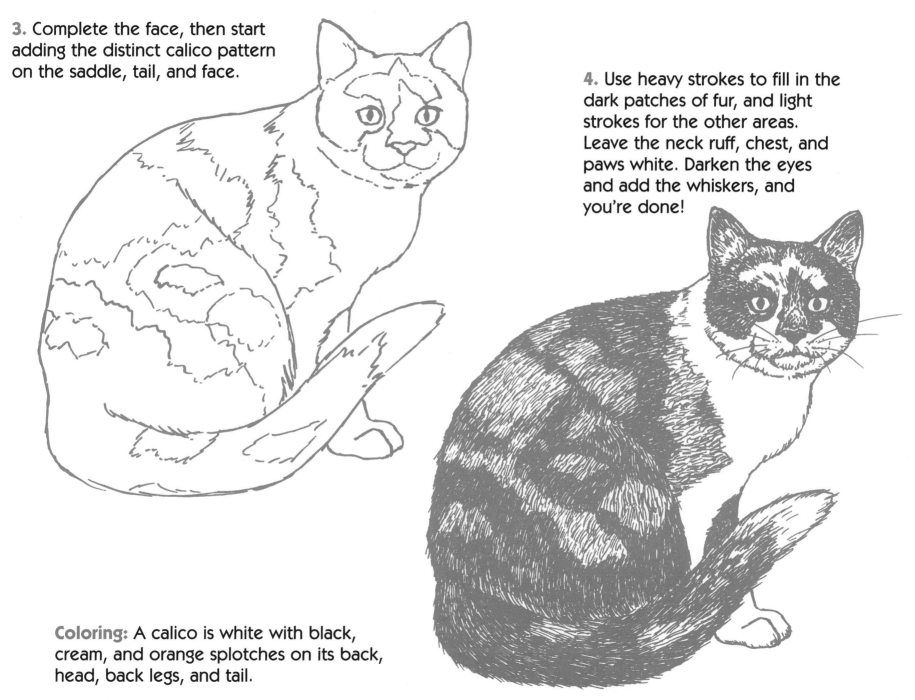

Coloring: A calico is white with black, cream, and orange splotches on its back, head, back legs, and tail.

Scottish Fold

This breed is known for its folded ears. Scottish folds are sweet-natured cats that adapt well to the environment of any home.

1. Start with a large free-form oval for the body. Add smaller ovals for the head, front shoulder, and hindquarters, as shown. Draw the lines for the chest. Then sketch the facial features, folded ears, and tail.

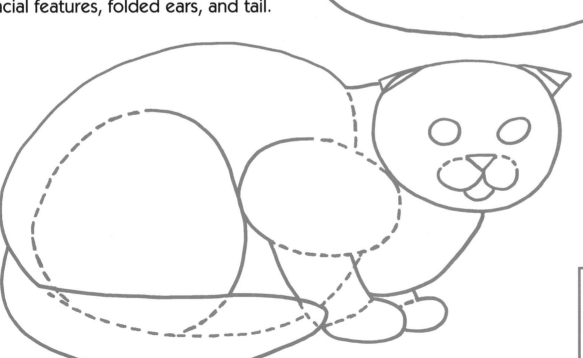

2. Create a smooth outline of the Scottish fold by sketching and erasing to blend all the shapes. Start to refine the facial features, erasing any lines you no longer need.

Remember: Studying the step 4 drawing before you begin will help you understand how the various shapes relate to each other.

3. Add the stripes and patches to the face. Darken the outline of the eyes and add the pupils. Use squiggly lines to mark the pattern on the body. Don't forget to add the toes.

4. Add whiskers. Then fill in the fur pattern, using long strokes for the body and short ones for the head. Follow the pattern as shown or make up your own. The folded ears define the breed, but the coat can be any color and pattern.

Coloring: A Scottish fold can be almost any color. You can make this one brown, rust, and white, or use your imagination.

Maine Coon

Maine coons cats are gentle creatures. They get along with children and other pets, including dogs, and enjoy playing in water. They are distinguished by their large, tufted ears and shaggy coat.

1. Start with overlapping ovals for the head and chest. Sketch the guideline body shape, as shown, then add long, narrow ovals to start the tail and foot. Start the facial features and pointy ears.

2. Blend the shapes together and refine the face, erasing unneeded lines. Create furry edges on the ears and the neck ruff. Add toes.

Remember: Don't be afraid to erase. Keep erasing and sketching until you are satisfied with your drawing at each step.

3. Add stripes and other markings to the face as shown. (For help, look for simple shapes —the *M* above the eyes, for example.) Darken the outline of the eyes and add the pupils. Use long and short strokes to create this cat's furry coat.

4. Use long, loose strokes to fill in the fur. (See page 5 for tips.) With a marker, darken the stripes on the face. Add the whiskers and your drawing will be complete.

Coloring: Maine coon cats can be any color.

Red Self

This longhaired breed's name used to be "orange," because of the color of its coat. The red self, which originated in Great Britain, has been around since the late 1800s.

1. Begin with a broad, oval head set on a heart-shaped chest. Add simple shapes for the hindquarters, legs, and feet. Then sketch the ears, facial features, and thick, bushy tail.

2. Sketch and erase to refine the basic body shape. Add to the facial features. Use jagged lines to create a furry outline for the face and chest. Draw toes.

Remember: It is easy to draw almost anything if you first break it down into simple shapes.

3. Darken the outline of the eyes and the pupil. Add the two upside-down *Y* shapes over the eyes. Then create the red self's fluffy coat by erasing sections of the body outline and replacing smooth lines with jagged lines or short, thick strokes.

4. Use a fine-tip marker to darken the face markings. Add the whiskers. Then use the marker, pencil, or crayons to create dark, shaggy fur all over this cat's face, body, and tail.

Coloring: The red self is a rusty red with darker rust markings and a lighter mask (markings around the eyes).

Russian Blue

This elegant shorthaired cat has long slim legs that are slightly longer in the back than in the front. Russian blues are good natured and intelligent.

1. Sketch simple guideline shapes for the head, chest, and hindquarters. Add guidelines for the ears and facial features, then sketch the body, legs, and tail.

2. Combine and round out the shapes to create a smooth outline of this cat. Erase any lines you no longer need as you sketch new ones.

Remember: Keep all lines and shapes lightly drawn until the final step.

3. Refine the ears and face, add pupils to the eyes, and sketch in the pattern on the face and body. Draw toes. Then sketch lots of very short lines, where shown, to create the fuzzy look of fur.

4. Now use lots short strokes to draw fur all over the body. Darken the eyes and the nose, then add other finishing touches.

Coloring: Russian blues are typically a bluish gray. For a more realistic look, use warm (reddish) and cool (bluish) grays and leave highlights —lighter areas—in the fur.

Bichon Frise

This curly-coated lapdog has soft, white, woolly fur. Frisky and affectionate, this dog's toylike appearance makes it a popular pet.

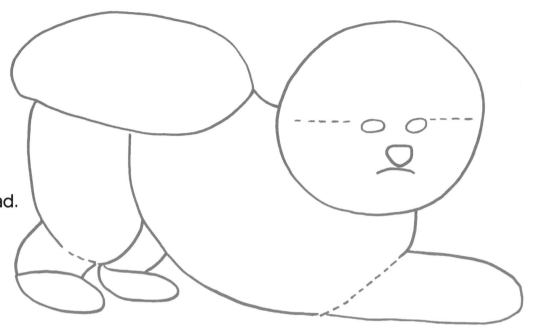

1. Begin with a large circle for the head. Add guidelines for the facial features. Then sketch free-form shapes for the body, tail, hindquarters, and legs.

Remember: If you are not satisfied with the way any part of your drawing looks, erase it and start over.

2. Blend the basic shapes, erasing any lines you no longer need. Rework the lines of the tail guideline shape to indicate fluffy fur. Then add ears and jowls on the head, as shown. Sketch a little ball for the bichon frise to play with.

3. Now use jagged edges to create fur all over this dog's body, including its face.

4. Darken the nose and eyes, but remember to leave a sparkle in each eye. Further fluff the fur on the head and body by using short strokes. Use longer strokes for the tail.

Coloring: The thick, wavy coat of a bichon frise is always white.

Chihuahua

Despite its small size, this lively dog knows no fear, even around dogs that are much bigger. The Chihuahua is also known as the Mexican hairless.

1. Begin by sketching the ovals for the head, chest, and hind-quarters. Next, sketch triangles for the large ears, and guideline shapes for the eyes and nose. Then sketch the legs, paws, and tail.

Remember: Study the step 4 picture before you start to draw.

2. Sketch and erase to combine the shapes into a smooth body outline. As you work, erase guidelines you no longer need. Add the muzzle and start refining the ears and facial features. Define the chest, belly, and hindquarters.

3. Sketching lightly, draw outlines showing where patches of white fur will appear. Further define the face, chest, and shoulder, then sketch in the toes.

4. Now you are ready to add the finishing touches. Use a sharp pencil or fine-tip marker to fill in the dark areas of this dog's fur, as shown. Darken the nose and eyes, leaving a bright spot in each eye.

Coloring: Chihuahuas vary in color, but typically they are cream and white.

Mixed-breed Puppy

All puppies are blind and helpless at birth. After one to two weeks, their eyes open and they begin to explore the world around them. Play is important to puppies. It helps them develop and, when playing with other puppies, teaches them how to get along with each other.

1. Start by lightly sketching an oval for a head, then add over-lapping free-form shapes for the ears and chest. Next, draw connecting lines and shapes for the legs, belly, hindquarters, and tail. Then sketch guideline shapes for the facial features.

2. Refine the shape of this puppy's head and body by sketching new lines as you erase unneeded ones. Fit the legs into the body and add toes to the paws. Keep revising until you have a clean, smooth outline.

3. Further define the details of this puppy's head and body. Note the patch around the left eye, and wrinkles on the chest and belly. Roughen some of the lines, as shown, to give the outline a furry look.

Remember: Focus on one section of the body at a time, erasing and redrawing until you are satisfied with it.

4. Use lots of short strokes to fill in the fur, then use a crayon or marker to color the dark patches. Darken the eyes, nose, and ears. Don't forget that puppies are usually fatter and have more wrinkles than adult dogs.

Coloring: Mixed-breed dogs can be of any color and have any sort of fur pattern and markings.

Afghan Hound

This breed is best known for its long, silky coat and long, floppy ears. Originally bred to be hunters, Afghans are agile, independent, and lively creatures.

1. Lightly sketch a circle for the head. Attach a large, free-from shape for the body and legs, as shown. On the head, sketch guideline shapes for the nose, muzzle, eye, and ear. Then add a tail.

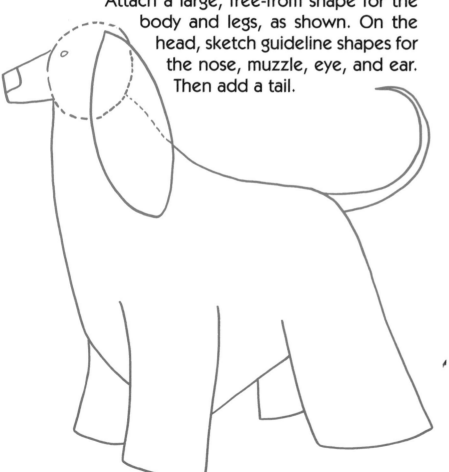

2. Erase and redraw to define the facial features, neck, and ears. Use slightly jagged lines on the legs and belly to indicate this dog's long, shaggy coat.

Tip: Practice makes perfect. Don't be discouraged if you don't get the hang of it right away. Just keep erasing and drawing until you do.

4. Working slowly and carefully, draw long, thin, wavy strokes for the ear and body fur and shorter strokes for the tail. Add the finishing touches—note, for instance, the darker face and saddle. Add some color or a background, and your drawing will be complete.

Coloring: The coat of an Afghan hound usually is all one color—often, shades of brown. The face and other markings may be darker, while the chest is more pale.

3. Refine the face and muzzle. Then continue reworking the outline of the body to show the length of the Afghan hound's long coat. Leave the paws visible under the shaggy legs.

Siberian Husky

Siberian huskies have extra-thick fur that protects them from the bitter Arctic cold. Known for their strength and persistence, these dogs are able to pull sleds for long distances. They are friendly and make good pets.

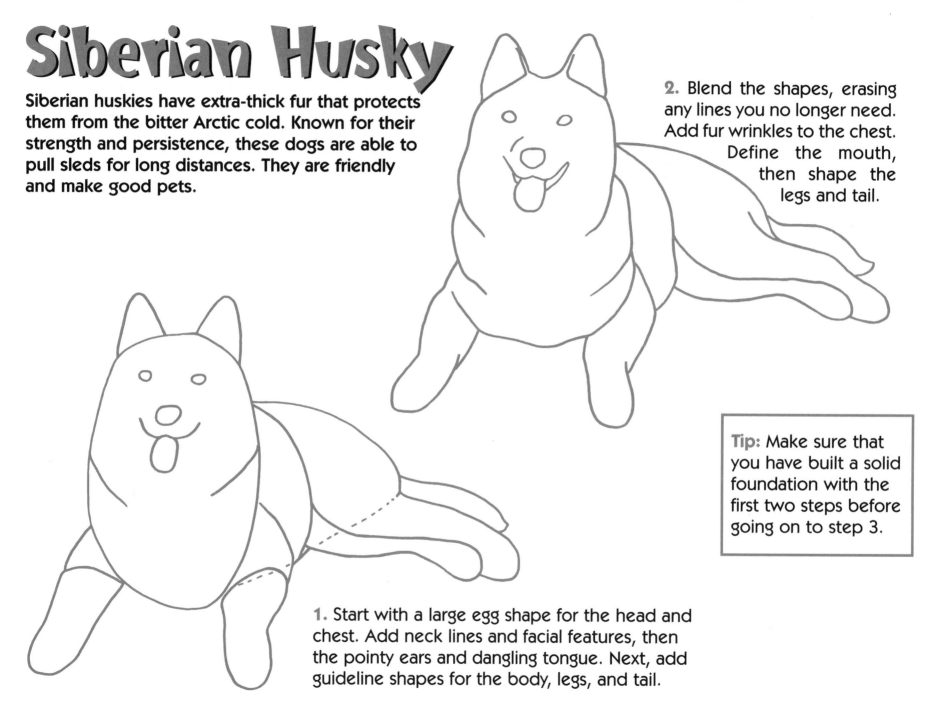

2. Blend the shapes, erasing any lines you no longer need. Add fur wrinkles to the chest. Define the mouth, then shape the legs and tail.

Tip: Make sure that you have built a solid foundation with the first two steps before going on to step 3.

1. Start with a large egg shape for the head and chest. Add neck lines and facial features, then the pointy ears and dangling tongue. Next, add guideline shapes for the body, legs, and tail.

3. Use a lot of very short, choppy lines to create a furry look for the outline of the head, body, and tail. Add toes and claws. Then sketch a furry-edged border for the white patches on the face and body.

4. For the finishing touches, use a marker or crayon to shade in the dark patches on the fur. (See page 5 on tips for giving the fur a realistic look.)

Coloring: Siberian huskies are white, black and white, or cream and white. Their eyes can be brown, crystal blue, or one of each.

Cocker Spaniel Puppy

Although golden-colored cocker spaniels are the most common, this breed can be any solid color, or even spotted. These friendly dogs have long, shaggy fur on the ears and underside.

2. Sketch and erase to combine the basic shapes into a clean, smooth outline. Define the ears and face, adding puppy wrinkles to the muzzle. Use squiggly lines to give the outline a furry look.

1. Lightly sketch a large, free-form shape for the body. Then sketch basic guideline shapes for the head, facial features, and ears. Add the legs and stubby tail.

Remember: Guidelines should always be lightly drawn, so they will be easy to erase when you no longer need them.

3. Further refine the facial features. Add all the little lines around the eyes and muzzle. Define the ears, chest, body and legs, then continue to rework all edges to make this puppy's shaggy coat look soft and fluffy.

4. Use light, quick, curving lines to create soft, curly fur all over this puppy's face and body. Add the final details —such as darkening the eyes and nose—and finishing touches to complete your drawing.

Coloring: Cocker spaniels are reddish brown, black, black and white, or brown and white.

Beagle

This small, short-haired hound is one of the oldest breeds of hunting dogs.

Remember: If a picture seems complex, look for the basic shapes and simple lines within it.

1. Begin by drawing three large, overlapping guideline shapes—for the head, chest, and hindquarters. Add legs, paws, and tail. Next, sketch the triangular ears and guideline shapes for the eyes and muzzle.

2. Carefully blend all the shapes into a clean, smooth outline. Add the toes. Refine the shape of the ears. As you work, erase any guidelines you no longer need.

4. Use a marker or crayon to shade the patches in the direction of fur growth. Draw claws on the toes, then darken the eyes and nose. Your beagle is ready to follow an interesting scent.

Coloring: Beagles are golden brown, reddish brown, or black, with white markings on the face, legs, belly, and chest. Most have a patch on the saddle.

3. Further define the facial features. Sketch outlines for the areas on the muzzle, chest, and legs that you will leave white. Add the folds to the ears. Now you are ready for the fun part—adding the finishing touches.

Old English Sheepdog

This breed was used to handle sheep and cattle in 18th-century England. It makes the perfect pet, because it is friendly as well as a good watchdog.

2. Erase and redraw to blend the lines and shapes into a clear outline. Erase unneeded guidelines. Then use choppy or jagged lines to start creating the shaggy coat. Define the mouth.

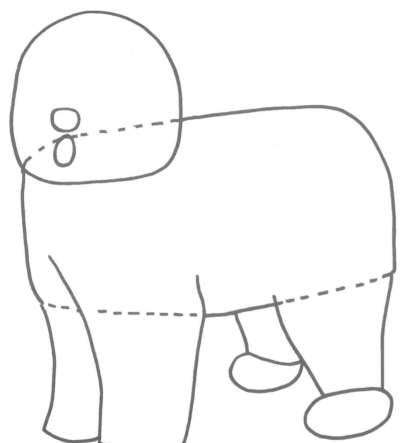

1. Lightly sketch a large free-form shape for the body. Add a smaller one for the head. Sketch in guideline shapes for the nose and tongue. (The eyes are behind shaggy fur.) Add legs and back paws.

Remember: Take your time doing steps 1 and 2. If you get the foundation right, the rest of your drawing will be easier to do.

3. Use many more jagged edges along the outline to make this sheepdog's coat thick and furry.

4. Darken the nose and define the tongue. Then, working carefully, sketch heavy strokes to shade in the dark areas and light strokes for the white areas. Add the finishing touches to complete your sheepdog.

Coloring: The old English sheepdog's long, shaggy coat is gray and white.

Pembroke Welsh Corgi

This breed was used for herding cattle because of its speed and agility. Welsh Corgis are loyal, affectionate, and very friendly.

1. Draw overlapping ovals for the corgi's head, neck, and chest. To the head, add simple shapes for the muzzle, eyes, and ears. Don't forget the tongue sticking out of the mouth. Sketch the body, then add the short legs and the paws.

2. Sketch and erase to blend your guideline shapes. Notice the curving lines for the skin folds at the neck, chest, and shoulders. Refine the facial features, adding the mouth and extending the tongue.

3. Sketch the pattern on the corgi's face. Use fuzzy lines to add fur definition as shown. Add in the toes. Now you are ready for the finishing touches.

> **Remember:** Do not add final details or finishing touches until your main figure is complete and you are satisfied with it.

4. Use lots of short strokes to create the short fur of this dog's coat. (See page 5 for tips on how to do this.) Notice that there are lots more fur lines in the dark areas, only a few in the white ones. Complete your drawing by adding a few lines on the chest and legs to indicate shadows.

Coloring: Pembroke Welsh corgis are black and tan, or reddish brown or gray-brown. Some, like this one, have white markings on the chest and legs.

Wirehaired Fox Terrier

Fox terriers are full of energy. Originally developed for fox hunting, they make very loving and protective pets. There are two types: wirehaired and smooth-haired.

2. Revise and blend your guideline shapes to form a clean outline of this dog's body. Erase lines you no longer need. Add the mouth and further define the head.

1. First sketch two large guideline shapes for the front legs. Add the squarish body and back-leg shapes. Sketch a brick shape for the head and a neck line. Then add the ears, eyes, nose, and tail.

Tip: Often, the easiest way to start a drawing is to sketch the largest shape first.

3. Use lots of short, choppy lines to give the head and body a furry look. Lightly sketch a furry-looking border for this dog's dark saddle patch.

4. Add details and patches of shading to complete this fox terrier. Carefully sketch in the curly hair using short, curved strokes. Darken the nose and eye, but leave the sparkle.

Coloring: Fox terriers are white with markings that are black or black and tan.

Dalmatian Puppy

Dalmatians are easily identified by the black spots on their white coats. They are best known as firehouse dogs.

2. Sketching lightly, blend the step 1 lines and shapes into a smooth outline of this puppy's body. As you work, erase lines you no longer need.

1. Begin by drawing a large free-form body shape, as shown. Sketch an oval head, with neck lines connecting it to the body. Add shapes for the legs, ears, facial features, and tail.

Remember: It is important to build a good foundation before refining your drawing.

3. Refine the face and ears. Add lines on the body as shown, to indicate folds in the puppy's skin. When you are satisfied with your drawing at this point, start adding the final touches.

4. Leave most of the coat white, but draw some fine lines for shading (see the ears, neck, and belly). Then add spots in a random pattern, varying the size and shape. Darken the nose and the eyes, and you're done!

Coloring: Dalmatians are white with black or brown spots.

Golden Retriever

Golden retrievers, like all retrievers, love to swim. This breed's beautiful, golden coat and good nature make it a household favorite.

1. Lightly sketch ovals for the upper body, then the head and hindquarters. Connect the two main body parts. Sketch guideline shapes for the muzzle and ear. Then add the legs, paws, and tail. (This golden retriever is taking a nap, so its eye is closed.)

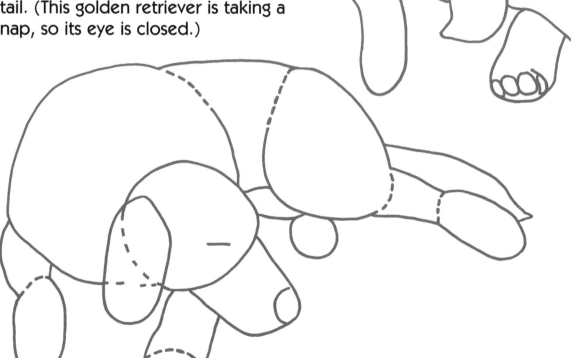

2. Sketch and erase, one area at a time, to reshape your guidelines into a more doglike shape. Curve and smooth the lines and shapes together, erasing those you no longer need. Sketch ovals for the paw pads. If you wish, add a collar.

3. Begin to create furlike lines around the body, as shown. (Don't forget the ear or the tail!) Then add toes and paw pads.

Remember: If at any point you don't like the way something looks, erase it and try again.

4. Use short strokes to make this dog's fur look full and fluffy all over. Add the finishing touches and you will have a happily napping golden retriever.

Coloring: The golden retriever's soft, shiny, wavy coat is a blend of yellow, gold, and orange.

Mixed-breed Dog (Mutt)

This drawing shows the illustrator's own dog—a hound/shepherd mix named Casey—sitting pretty.

1. Draw a free-form shape for the head and chest, then others for the lower body and back leg. Sketch a square muzzle. Add the eye and ear. Then attach the legs and tail.

2. Blend the guideline shapes into a clean, smooth outline, erasing any lines you no longer need. Add the nose and mouth shapes. Start refining the shape of the ear and muzzle.

3. In this drawing, the artist sketched in a pattern for dark patches on the saddle and tail. However, feel free to change the pattern to whatever you want. (This will be *your* dog!) Just be sure to create a furry outline. Add toes and paw pads.

4. Slowly and carefully shade in the pattern using short strokes. You can be creative with the finishing touches to make your own "unique" dog.

Coloring: The artist's mixed-breed dog is reddish brown and black, but you can make yours any color you wish.

Remember: Always feel free to use your imagination when adding the final touches.

Puli

The puli is famous for its unusual coat. Cordlike strands cover the entire body, hiding the facial features and making it look more like a walking mop than a dog.

1. Draw a large, free-form shape for this dog's body. Add an overlapping oval for the head. Then sketch a guideline shape for the floppy tail.

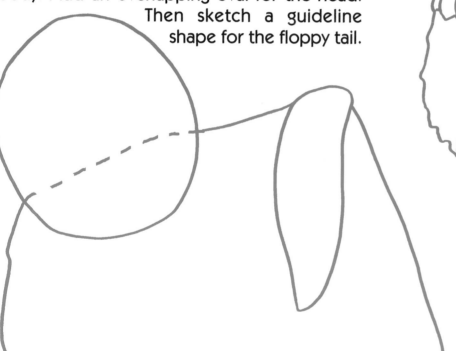

2. Sketch and erase to reshape the body, head, and tail to suggest the ends of this dog's long, cordlike coat. Add a neck ruff with similar edges. Then add the nose and extended tongue. (You can't see the eyes or any other facial features, because they are hidden behind the long, corded hair.)

3. Add the tongue and nose details. Then get busy: You have a lot of coat to create! Starting at the top of the head, draw the long cords of fur. Then do the tail, then the rest of the body. This may look hard to do, but be patient and carefully sketch one cord at a time, and you will do fine.

> **Remember:** When something seems complex, look at it another way. Break it down into simple, basic shapes and try drawing those.

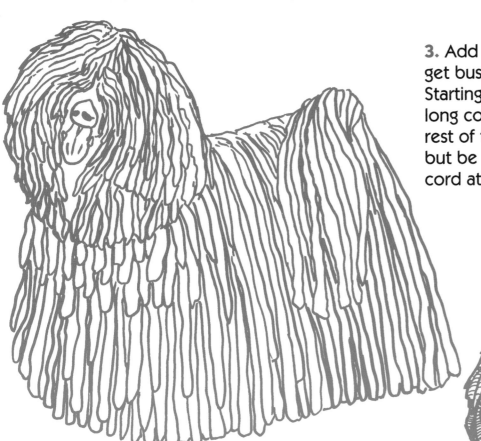

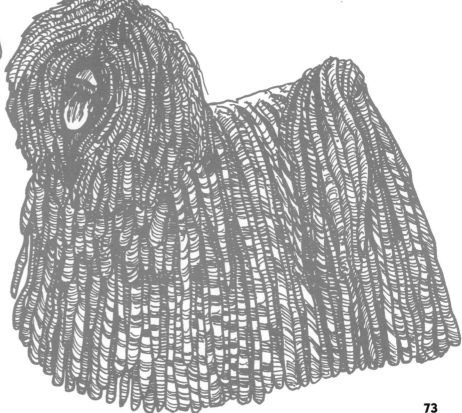

4. Using short strokes—some thick, some thin—add the final details to your cording. Draw different degrees of detail on each cord, depending on how you want *your* puli to look. Complete the nose and tongue.

Coloring: Most pulis are black with gray or yellowish brown highlights. Some are all white or all gray.

Pug

The pug is one of the oldest dog breeds. Pugs probably originated in China, and may have been pets in Buddhist monasteries in Tibet. Pugs make very good pets, because they are loving and don't require much exercise or grooming.

1. Start by lightly sketching an oval chest, then a squarish head. Draw the legs, paws, and bean-shaped tail. Then add ears and guideline shapes for the facial features.

2. Erase and redraw to blend the shapes into a smooth pug outline, as shown. Erase unnecessary lines as you define the legs, shoulder, and neck. Refine the facial features, shaping the muzzle and big chin. Define the shape of the tail.

Remember: Keep erasing and redrawing until you are satisfied with the way your drawing looks.

3. Draw wrinkles on this dog's face, chest, and saddle. Add lines to the chest to define the powerful muscles there. Get this stage of the drawing just right before going on the finishing touches in step 4.

4. Darken the mask, ears, and eyes, but leave a little white spot in the eyes to give more life to your drawing. To complete your pug, add some shading, as shown.

Coloring: The pug is light brown, black, or silvery gray, with black face, ears, and saddle patch.

Shar-pei

The shar-pei is known for its wrinkly skin. The name is Chinese for "sand-fur" or "sand-skin." Shar-peis love humans and make good pets.

1. Begin by lightly drawing large guideline shapes for the chest and body. Add an oval for the head. Sketch free-form shapes for the legs, paw, and curled tail. Then sketch shapes for the ears, eye, muzzle, and nose.

2. Blend the shapes, erasing guidelines to create a smooth, clean outline of the legs and body. Refine the muzzle and other facial features. Reshape the ears and tail. Add muscle lines on the chest and shoulder.

Remember: Keep all your guidelines lightly drawn, so they will be easier to erase later.

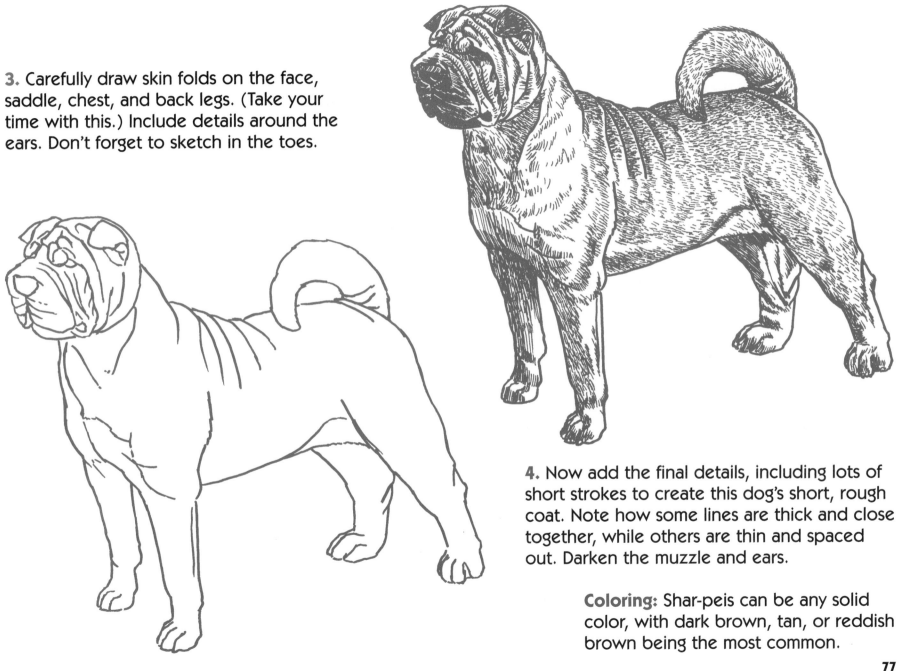

3. Carefully draw skin folds on the face, saddle, chest, and back legs. (Take your time with this.) Include details around the ears. Don't forget to sketch in the toes.

4. Now add the final details, including lots of short strokes to create this dog's short, rough coat. Note how some lines are thick and close together, while others are thin and spaced out. Darken the muzzle and ears.

Coloring: Shar-peis can be any solid color, with dark brown, tan, or reddish brown being the most common.

Bulldog

Bulldogs are good guard dogs, but they also make loving pets that are gentle with children.

1. Begin by drawing a large, free-form oval for the powerful chest. Add smaller guide-line shapes for the head and muzzle. (Note that the muzzle is shaped like an upside-down heart). Next, sketch the hindquarters, legs, and paws. Then add the eyes, ears, and nose.

2. Erase and redraw, one area at a time, to round the shapes. Blend them into a clean outline, erasing any lines you no longer need. Fit the lower jaw into the jowls. Create the toes.

Remember: Don't be afraid to erase. It usually takes a lot of drawing and erasing before you are satisfied with the way your drawing looks. Practice makes perfect!

78

3. Add all the face wrinkles. Lightly sketch outlines for the dark face markings and the white patches on this dog's chest and paws. Sketch lines on the neck to indicate loose skin. Notice how wide the chest is.

4. Use short lines to sketch in the fur, but leave some areas white. Darken the nose, eyes, and the ears. Add claws to the paws. With a few other finishing touches, as shown, your bulldog will almost pop off the page.

Coloring: Bulldogs are tan, white, or reddish brown, or white with patches of one of the darker colors.

Pekingese

In the past, the pekingese was considered a sacred animal, and a favorite pet of ancient China's royal family. Small but brave, these long-haired dogs make loyal pets.

1. Lightly sketch a large oval for the head and chest area. Add simple shapes for the muzzle, eyes, and ears. Draw other free-form shapes for the body, front paws, back leg, and tail.

2. Blend all the shapes together, creating a jagged outline to show the ends of this dog's very long fur. Add toes to the front paw.

3. Darken the muzzle, nose, and eyes. Leave a little white spot in each eye. Use long strokes to add fur detail to the rest of the body. Add other finishing touches to complete your sketch.

Coloring: The pekingese is usually golden tan or another light color, and always has a black face mask.

Samoyed

This breed of dog is known for its "smile." Samoyeds are lively, intelligent creatures that need a lot of exercise. They are friendly toward everyone—even intruders!

1. Start with a large egg-shaped oval for the head and chest. Add facial features and ears. Draw free-form shapes for the body, legs, and paws. Don't forget the curled tail.

2. Sketch and erase to define the overall body, as shown. Do the same for the face, ears, paws, and tail.

3. Samoyeds have very fluffy fur. Create it by carefully drawing lots of jagged or choppy lines over the outline of the body. Darken the nose and eyes, then add other final details to complete your drawing.

Coloring: The samoyed's coat is snow white, cream, or pale gray. The eyes and nose are black. Add a slightly darker color in the shadow areas (under the chest and belly) for a realistic look.

German Shepherd

These dogs, also known as Alsatians, originally worked as farm dogs in Germany. Easily trained, they are used as guard dogs, guides for the blind, and assistants to search-and-rescue teams and the police. They also are popular as pets.

1. Lightly sketch a large oval for the body, then a smaller one for the head. Next, sketch simple shapes to start the eyes, ears, nose, muzzle, and floppy tongue. Then add the legs, paws, and tail.

2. Blend the shapes, erasing lines you no longer need. Define the ears and the facial features. Use choppy or jagged lines to look like fur on the shoulders and chest. Add toes. This German shepherd is sitting, so its visible hind leg is folded and shaped like a drumstick.

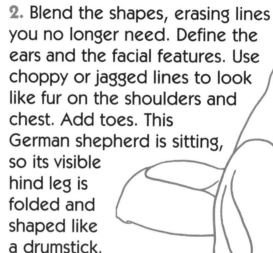

Tip: This drawing may seem complicated. Be patient, and break each step down into smaller ones. Follow along carefully, and you will be amazed at how easy it turns out to be.

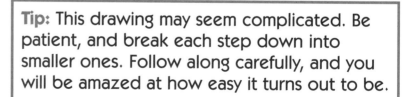

3. Start adding details to the face, including outlines for the dark patches you will create around the eyes and on the muzzle. Refine the toes and add claws. Continue to work on most of the body lines to show this dog's dense, coarse fur.

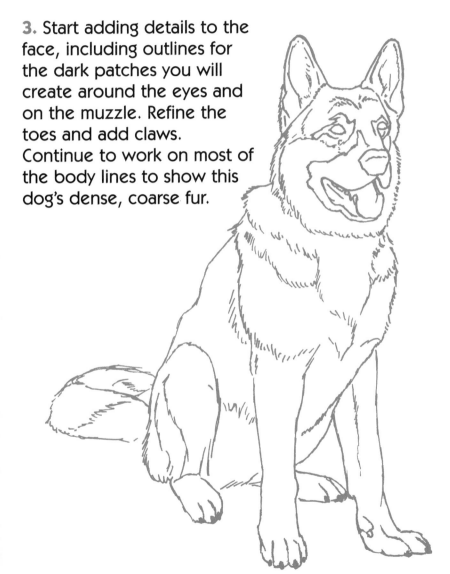

4. Now add the final details to your drawing. Use a marker or heavy pencil strokes to shade in the dark patches. Create fuzzy edges for the fur and add finishing touches to the face.

Coloring: This breed's saddle, inner ears, muzzle, and mask around the eyes are black. The rest of the body is usually tan and black, with a lighter color on the belly. On some German shepherds, reddish brown or pale gray is the main body color.

Black Labrador Retriever

The Labrador retriever is an excellent hunting dog, especially when hunting waterfowl (such as ducks). Like other retrievers, it is strong, solid, and friendly.

2. Carefully blend the lines and shapes into a smooth outline of the Labrador retriever. As you work, erase any lines you no longer need. Refine the ears and facial features. Add the skin flaps on the neck and wrinkles on the body. Then draw a soft pillow for the Lab to lie on.

1. Start by lightly drawing ovals for this dog's head and chest. Add triangles for ears, small ovals for eyes, and other simple shapes for the muzzle. Then sketch free-form shapes for the body, legs, and tail. Note that this has its front legs crossed.

3. Continue to refine this dog's body and add details to the face, as shown. Sketch patches for where the fur will be lighter. Add the collar and claws.

Remember: Keep all your lines lightly drawn until you get to the final stages.

4. Although this Labrador retriever is all black, your sketch will look more realistic if you leave light areas in the fur. Leave lots of white spaces between the black areas, showing the way light reflects off the dark fur. Use a marker or crayon to shade in the dark areas.

Coloring: Black Labrador retrievers have blue highlights in their black fur. Lightly color with blue before putting the black strokes over the top. Leave the highlights white. Some Labs have dark brown or yellowish brown fur.

Dachshund

This dog is known for its unusual shape and is often called the "hot dog" or "sausage dog." Dachshunds are lively and intelligent, and make good watchdogs despite their small size. They were once used as hunting dogs. (The word *dachshund* is German for "badger dog.")

1. Begin by drawing a large oval for the chest, then add a long free-form oval for the rest of the body. Next, sketch a guideline shape for the head, as shown. Add simple shapes for the eyes, nose, and large floppy ears. Then sketch the tail, legs, and paws.

2. Sketch, erase, and redraw to combine all the shapes into a clean, smooth outline of this dachshund's body. Define the head, ears, and long muzzle. Add the lines on the chest to indicate muscle.

Tip: Step 2 is very important, so take your time with it. It establishes the basic structure and overall look of your drawing. In steps 3 and 4, you will simply refine and add details to what you created in step 2.

3. Continue to refine this dog's facial features, then start adding other details, such as lines to represent the folds around the front legs, shoulders, and chest. Don't forget to draw in the toes.

4. With a marker, use tiny strokes to create the dachshund's short fur. Note that the muzzle, eyebrows, belly, and feet are a lighter color. Leave a nice sparkle in the eye, then add the finishing details to complete this friendly dog.

Coloring: This dog's fur is one of three types: smooth-haired, wirehaired, or long-haired. The dachshund is usually reddish brown or tan and black.

Rottweiler

The rottweiler is one of the strongest and most powerful breeds of dogs. Rottweilers are often used as guard dogs or police dogs. Although they tend to be aggressive, with proper training, Rottweilers can also make good and loyal pets.

1. Lightly sketch a large oval shape for the chest. Add freeform shapes for the head and body. Add legs and paws, then work on the head—lightly sketch guideline shapes for the ears, eyes, muzzle, and extended tongue. Don't forget the short tail.

2. Combine the shapes, erasing guidelines you no longer need. Define the outline of the legs and body. Refine the shape of the muzzle and mouth. Add toes.

Remember: It is easy to draw almost anything if you first break it down into simple shapes.

3. Continue refining the body. (Note the wrinkle lines in the face, and at the neck and shoulder.) Define the toes and draw small triangles for the teeth. Then, sketching lightly, draw guidelines for where you will create lighter-colored patches in this dog's coat.

4. Using a fine-tip marker, make short strokes to shade in the fur. Create light areas on the back and around the neck by leaving more room between the strokes. Use heavy strokes with a marker or crayon to create the darkest areas. Then add the final details, such as the tongue and eyes.

Coloring: The rottweiler's coat is black, with tan patches on the face, chest, and legs.

Miniature Pinscher

The miniature pinscher (min pin), is a loyal and intelligent dog. It is known for its courage and is an expert at catching rats.

1. Start with a large, free-form shape for the chest. Add an oval head. Sketch triangles for the large pointy ears, and guideline shapes for the eyes and muzzle. Next, sketch shapes for the body, legs, paws, and short tail.

2. Revise and blend the guideline shapes, erasing unneeded lines. Define the ears and facial features.

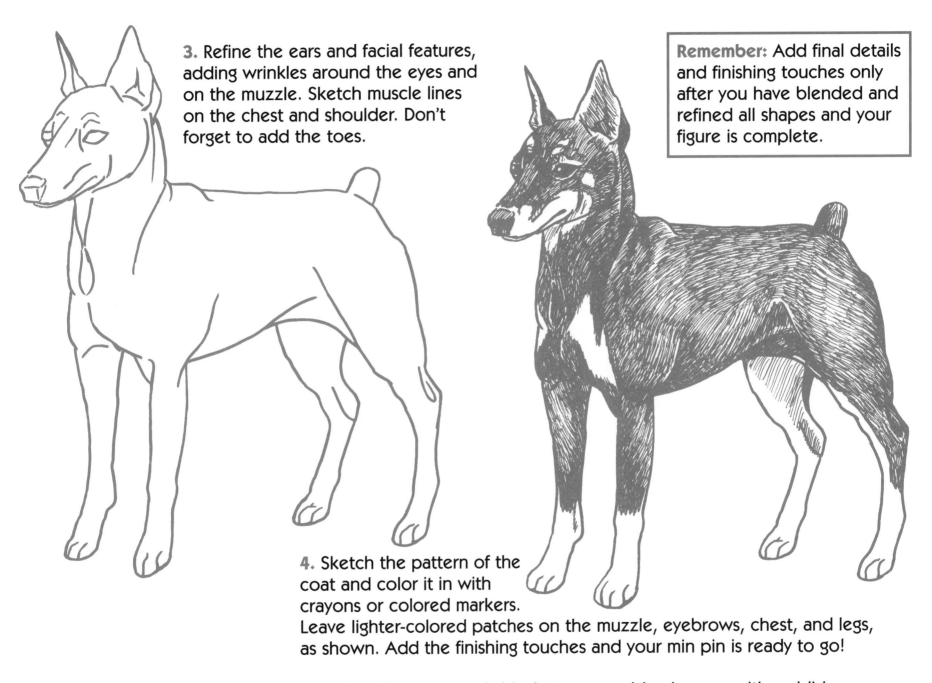

3. Refine the ears and facial features, adding wrinkles around the eyes and on the muzzle. Sketch muscle lines on the chest and shoulder. Don't forget to add the toes.

Remember: Add final details and finishing touches only after you have blended and refined all shapes and your figure is complete.

4. Sketch the pattern of the coat and color it in with crayons or colored markers.
Leave lighter-colored patches on the muzzle, eyebrows, chest, and legs, as shown. Add the finishing touches and your min pin is ready to go!

Coloring: The pinscher is black, tan, or golden brown, with reddish brown areas on the face, chest, tail, and legs.

INDEX

Cats

Abyssinian
page 17

American Shorthair
pages 22-23

Angora
pages 8-9

Burmese
pages 34-35

Calico
pages 36-37

Devon Rex
pages 14-15

Kittens Playing
pages 28-31

Korat
pages 20-21

Longhaired Silver Tabby
pages 16

Maine Coon Cat
pages 40-41

Manx
pages 18-19

Persian
pages 32-33

Red Self
pages 42-43

Russian Blue
pages 44-45

Scottish Fold
pages 38-39

Siamese
pages 24-25

Sphynx
page 7

Tabby Cat
pages 26-27

Tortoiseshell
pages 10-11

Turkish Van
pages 12-13

Dogs

Afghan Hound
pages 52-53

Beagle
pages 58-59

Bichon Frise
pages 46-47

Black Labrador Retriever
pages 84-85

Bulldog
pages 78-79

Chihuahua
pages 48-49

Cocker Spaniel Puppy
pages 56-57

Dachshund
pages 86-87

Dalmatian Puppy
pages 66-67

German Shepherd
pages 82-83

Golden Retriever
pages 68-69

Miniature Pinscher
pages 90-91

Mixed-breed Dog (Mutt)
pages 70-71

Mixed-breed Puppy
pages 50-51

Old English Sheepdog
pages 60-61

Pekingese
page 80

Pembroke Welsh Corgi
pages 62-63

Pug
pages 74-75

Puli
pages 72-73

Rottweiler
pages 88-89

Samoyed
page 81

Shar-pei
pages 76-77

Siberian Husky
pages 54-55

Wirehaired Fox Terrier
pages 64-65